The Unlived-lives
of Dora Wunbery
and other poems

by
Satyalila Jen Brown

Published 2013 by
Garret Hermitage Publications
The Shed
89 Sommerville Road
BS7 9AE

ISBN 978-1-291-29350-0
Printed by Lulu

Acknowledgments

'Dora Wunbery', 'Mum', 'Finding her Apron; and 'Transaction' first appeared in "FWBO New Poetry 2000", Rising Fire Press, 2000

'Puzzle', 'On the train to Basingstoke' and 'Transaction' were subsequently published in "The Heart as Origami", Rising Fire press, 2005

'An Average Wednesday' was first published in 'The Poet's Way' by Manjusvara, Windhorse Publications, 2011

Credits

Cover design by Ananda (Stephen Parr)
Front cover photo "Plate and fablon in the Garret" by Satyalila, 2012
Back cover photo "Satyalila at Pendine Sands, 1 January 2013 " by Prajnagupta 2013

for Dora & Ivy

Contents

The Unlived-lives of Dora Wunbery
Poems 2002-2012

Big Kauri

Twice I'd set out and turned back.
I wanted to visit this god of the land.

Town-bred timidity kept me on well-worn paths,
but the third time I knew: I had to go on.

Fascination drew me. Twisting
and turning through treeferns and log-falls

I clambered down steeply, clutching at roots,
till I saw with my heart what the camera could not:

a vast and living citadel of grey bark,
smooth and rising sheer with leaves so far

and ferns and orchids sprawling
in a wide spread of branches -

higher than my eye could reach,
wider than my arms, older than my life.

I stood still before it
then sat at its feet.

Sudarshanaloka (New Zealand), October 2002

Yoshizawa's Pigeon and other possibilities

> *"...their folding of anatomically correct*
> *insects and sea creatures, complete*
> *with all their legs and other*
> *appendages, finally proved that the*
> *possibilities of an uncut square of*
> *paper were limitless."*

Two weeks alone in an old caravan on a Welsh hillside.
I was definitely ironed out –
creases still visible, but not worn through.

Nick, the gardener, had told me about butterflies –
how in the chrysalis, utterly surrendered to change,
some liquefy so that even stuck with a pin, there's no pain.

Resisting dissolution, yet bent on change, I considered
the choices I could make - crane, salt cellar, Japanese lady?
Ostrich? Elephant? Swan?

> *"If you fold carelessly, the result will be disastrous."*

Vajrakuta Caravan (Wales), October 2010

Most marvellous of all milk-bottle tops

I could see the mounds and folds
of cumulus made bright by your light.
I could not see you, then.

Later on as I was making tea,
you stopped me, reached
right through the glass, singing.

I walked outside in my slippers,
stood gazing up at you
smiling at the stars.

I looked. I squinted. I frowned.
I tried to see you as the sphere you are –
I failed. You gleamed back,

ever-so brightly; a shiny disc of tin-foil
stuck on the flat black
curtain of the sky.

Taraloka (Shropshire) and Bristol, September 2008 – May 2012

Ashes

for Manjusvara

I have to confess I was tempted
to unscrew the pot and take a pinch of you.

The red plastic urn was on top of my bookshelf.
I'd fetched you from the Co-op on Gloucester Road –

or rather fetched the *third* you'd designated
- you divvied out yourself so equably.

I carried you in the discrete purple gift-bag they supplied
to the Buddhist Centre, where I put you on my desk.

That didn't seem quite right,
so I moved you to the shrine,

then brought you home with me, on the bus.
This is one of many things I imagine telling you – after.

Bristol, August 2011

Security

Wedged between Stubbington Avenue and Laburnum Grove,
our road was terraced - 'parlour entrances' down the *other* end,
but in our section, hallways, forecourts, standard roses.

Our red-brick house had woodwork painted murky green,
black gate and railings – fifties replacements
for the ones given up in the war.

Many of the fences shared a familiar pattern of curly scrolls,
but on our gate the centre-bottom curl was bent,
almost to straightness, by my swinging Clarks-shod feet.

For fear of peeling paint, a wide-striped canvas curtain
was hung up in the porch and brought in at dusk.
At midnight, when the telly screen had faded to a dot,

the milk checks were put out, the bolts slid into the flimsy frame,
and the upturned lucky horse-shoe was left in the dark,
hanging on its ribbon of faded tartan, just inside the door.

Bristol, 2008-2012

Dinner Time

I

The rising whistle said "I'm home", the falling reply
said "Hi". Each dinner time he lumbered in -
helmet, great-coat and steel-capped boots:
smelling of oil, stale with sweat.

He hung his coat on the front-room door,
put his helmet on the coffee table.
Heavy steps up the long passage,
he sat with a creak in his carver chair.

Dinner was always "on the table at twelve."
Baked potatoes and cold meat Monday,
shepherd's pie Tuesday, chop roast Wednesday,
steak and kidney Thursday…

He liked a lot of gravy.
Heaving himself from his chair
he'd wheeze across the room
to fetch a spoon from the chest of drawers.

Straight after, we had cups of tea –
he had to be back at the 'Yard by one.
He'd stop to catch the lunchtime news
and then bend down to kiss her as he left.

Her day: a matrix of meals and tea,
of washing, cleaning, going to the shops.
She was held in such a mesh of love;
she couldn't breathe.

Getting the dinner ready for us by noon:
Me, home from school, Dad from the 'Yard
and Aunty, back from the Coop.
A brief oasis after this,

her paper and a cigarette or two.
An hour she'd take, to sit there
for herself. Her wooden carver chair
cornered by the dresser

whose wide shelf held her clutter:
maps saved from the Mail on Sunday
the rack of place-mats, views of Venice.
Letters from Mary, drawings from the kids,

her Boots "Home" Diary, crossword pen,
my school reports, a book of Coop stamps,
her puffer, Lambert & Butlers and
the un-read Parish News.

Returning home on Sundays, twenty-something,
I would do the washing up.
I'd wipe and stow it all away
while she sat there (newspaper, fag).

And some days later, on the phone,
she'd say she liked the little chaos that I left –
the pan she couldn't find, the spoon,
the hidden mixing bowl, the pyrex jug.

Croydon and Bristol, 2000-2012

Dora Wunbery

Perhaps it was in a bid to break free
that my mother one day took hold
of her Audrey Brown self.
She turned it inside out
and with a few quick origami folds
made herself an anagram.

Don't ask me how
the Daily Mail reader still held supreme –
most days.
But then, sudden as a kingfisher,
I would catch a glimpse of fleeting Dora Wunbery
at mischief. Playing words

living the hum of life
with a wicked laugh
before suddenly she was caught
by the scorpion-tailed conservative voter
and pulled up short by the kite-string
hurtling her back to earth.

Croydon, March 1998

Dora and the Dandelions

I knew you watched them through the kitchen door,
positioning yourself to peer out of the one clear pane
that replaced the patterned glass we broke as kids.

You liked them and you didn't,
enjoyed their brightness, fretted for the lawn.
nipped out to pick them before they went to seed.

And now, for me, they matter still –
defiant yellow buttons, demonstrating
against the sensible concerns of ordinary life.

Croydon and Bristol, 1999 - 2010

Green and Roses

Stepping onto the escalator at Balham underground,
I remember how you used to pause,
looking bewildered at the dizzying stairs,
while I teased that you were waiting for your favourite.

The green-glazed tiles were 'you', as well -
your green, the colour of the carpet that you chose
to go with rose wallpaper, pink candlewick
and the Lloyd-loom box with the satin lid

in your Ideal Home Bedroom, circa 1956.
And suddenly, as I descend, I feel your hands,
just dried from washing up,
wiping my nose, tucking my vest in tight.

Croydon and Bristol, 2000-2007

Dora Wunbery Again

There you are again, reeling out smiles
of kite-string from the block and tackle
of the heart you gave me.

I sit on my table by the window.
There's a strong wind blowing in;
it knocks the window-cleaning liquid off the sill.

I'm wearing a going-out skirt,
not a working-at-home one.
You would not have approved.

The 'Art of Fugue', on harpsichord
is playing loudly – a musical anagram
of somebody else's name.

Because of you, I have put down my cloth
and scrunched up newspaper
to pick up a pencil.

"She only *ever* does the middle bit," you said.
"You should always start with the corners
and the middle will take care of itself."

Bristol, April 2010

Round the Street

She always went 'round the street' -
after the housework, before she cooked the lunch –
to get the shopping; maybe mince
or pork chops, a cauli from Mrs Gold.
She'd 'pay the papers', buy her ciggies
and, when she was older, fetch the pensions
or take prescriptions to Tremletts, where,
she said, they always 'spoke'.
After she died I went myself.
I went to say goodbye on her behalf –
to cancel papers, fill in forms.
To walk along past the Odeon and not go in.

Akashavana (Spain), June 2007

Eighteen Months Later

We finally pulled
the red cardboard suitcase from under her bed.

We emptied out her dressing-gown, her slippers
and the plastic box in which she kept her teeth.

The coins in her purse were tarnished with cold.
They didn't feel at all like currency.

I couldn't bring myself to tip them out –
to mix them up with ordinary cash.

I wished they had been buried at her side,
an ancient custom at the funeral of a queen.

Croydon, Bristol and Akashavana (Spain), 1999 – 2011

Through the Looking Glass

I licked my middle finger, began dabbing up the crumbs
from the otherwise empty plate, and then I jumped –
this *w*as *your* habit, *your* gesture.

I'd seen you do it dozens of times,
witnessed the crumb-free plates you left
lying around your bachelor pad.

Away from you for weeks,
was I manifesting you in habit-form?
And then I smiled, remembering quite another time –

my mother twelve years dead by then – when I first caught myself
narrowing my eyes, holding out a packet at arms' length,
tilting my head back, trying to focus tiny print.

The recognition, then, had dizzied me,
like I'd been tipped backwards through the looking glass –
seeing me see my mother do this squint.

Vajrakuta Caravan (Wales), October 2010

Living with Seagulls

Eight years I've lived
among these rooftops
full of screams.

Joy or hunger,
impatience or despair:
I still don't understand.

In spring
it's like they kick
the roof-tiles overhead.

My nearest neighbours,
rarely seen – occasionally
a large gull comes to stand

beside my open window.
At such times
I find myself afraid –

the beadiness of their eyes,
the solidity of their bodies.
Those great webbed orange feet.

Bristol, 2011-12

Full Moon Spoon

Jostled in a mug with other spoons,
this one – of hall-marked silver –
came to hand. I felt the fine-boned curves,
its crazed bowl, bright with years of use,

the bottom flat, the edges
thin as sharpened knives.
It was delicate as the form of a tiny bird.
And each time since, when I've been to that place

I look and hope to find it waiting there:
a childhood habit, to depend on things
being safely on the same shelf year after year.
But I have never seen that spoon again.

I cup my hands, can almost feel the shape;
the bird I thought I once felt flutter there has flown

Tiratanaloka (Wales) and Bristol, Full Moon Day, January 2007 – May 2012

Teaspoon Elegy

i.m. David Palmer, 15 October 1935 – 5 January 2010

All morning we'd been buttering bread, boiling eggs and lifting the cat
again and again out of the cardboard box intended for the sandwiches.
Finally, we ironed and brushed our clothes.

When we got to the hired room we remembered the teaspoons,
so I nipped round to Poundland (since Woolies had just shut down)
and got twenty for a fiver, only an hour before the hearse was due.

Helen, in her pinny, put on the urn, assembled his favourite train set
and laid out the cake: bara brith, ginger bread, and crisps.
Afterwards, we all drank tea and talked and watched:

the train went round and round. Then, later, as I wrapped
and packed the borrowed plates, she came. She handed me five
                                                    teaspoons,
shining, rough-edged, saint-apostles I carried home to my kitchen
                                                    drawer.

Aberystwyth and Bristol, January 2010 – June 2012

Two Wednesdays

An Average Wednesday:

And the usual number of poem images
went by like buses.
And again I forgot
to stick out my hand.

Another Wednesday:

Full-moon, lunar eclipse, invisible
behind a bank of cloud, and you,
my friend, fading, far away —
I raise my hand.

Dhanakosa (Scotland) June 2001 & Bristol, June 2011

Windfalls in Clifton Wood

for Manjusvara

Beneath the apple tree that sprawls
the high wall, I kneel over them.
They'd drawn me, across the street,
reminding me of you.

Every year you'd come to the class
in autumn, bringing carrier bags
of fallen eaters you'd gathered for us
from your Mum's garden.

The last time you called me back
as I was leaving - you were stood
at the side door in the dark
holding out my own special bag-full.

Today I search the bruised, worm-eaten fruit
and find one small, pink, perfect apple.
Rubbing it against my jersey, I walk on
till I come to a bench with a view.

Bristol, 2011-2012

Sindy's Sex Change

Pyrex. Ciggies. Duraglit.
Bonky. Albie. Sindy. Tut.
All these words, it claimed,
were simply my mistake.
It proffered the correction.

I could understand not-knowing
the name of Mary's albino goldfish
but to deny my famous, jet-set friend?
To be unaware of her immense wardrobe,
red sports car, handsome love-interest, Ken?

No. One careless click of a button
and the sex-change spell-checker
would have been at work across the globe,
in the bottom of wardrobes
and neglected cardboard boxes,

on every pink-frilled dressing table, plastic palace
and quilted bed, taking the poor girl
in its merciless binary hands,
creating a brave new world
of Sidney dolls.

Bristol, 4 May 2012

'Descent into Limbo' on the way to Sainsbury's

I totally missed Adam and I didn't spot Eve.
Never noticed the ivy leaves, the fig leaves
or the face that's hidden in the rock.
I didn't clock the discarded nails
laid in a cross shape on the ground.
Nor did I realise that there was a book
crushed beneath the broken-down door.

But, see, the one in white is leaning forward,
pulling somebody out of the dark?
The trumpet-blowing cherub looks annoyed,
but that other man beside him
is patiently holding his cross –
like any guy might hold another's tools,
while his mate just finishes off a job.

Bristol, 2011 – 2012
Based on 'Christ's descent into limbo' by Bellini, Bristol City Museum
and Art Gallery

Poems from 'Puzzle'

a collection self-published in 2001

Hang-gliding

In loving to stand
on Portsdown Hill
she taught me.

My memories now are made
of her dandelion delight
after long mornings

of ritual housework when,
in sudden flight, she rose
on lucid thermals.

Now that I am alone,
I seek some secret message
she might have left me, embedded

in the palms of my hands,
the curve of my spine. In this
unfathomable longing to fly.

April 1999

Mum

Regular as clockwork
and without the embarassed hesitation of grief,
her paper landed on the door mat.

Each morning I picked it up,
knew no-one would read it
and folded it neatly by her empty chair.

March 1998

Finding her Apron

Forgotten,
her apron held its counsel
behind the kitchen door.

Comings and goings of care-workers
saw to his needs, sanitised
traces of her as they reorganised
the kitchen.

Soft emblem of her status,
it hung there,
two pegs in the frayed pocket
since her last dash
to rescue the washing.

Breathing her presence,
I am a child at her knees again,
burying my face,
trying to hold on
so that she will not go.

June 1998

Yawning Freedom

Yawning tracts
of freedom lie ahead.
The last of my roots pulled up
as he let go the tenuous grip
of his veiny hand.

I am left walking,
step by careful step
towards an unknown future,
judge and witness gone,
my anchor freed.

June 1998

The Ways of Sadness

(after Ananda)

I am learning the ways of sadness.
How it falls like a gentle darkness
once a quietness is made for it.

How it can be
a softly enfolding cloak
if I will only wear it.

I am learning its names,
how it hides and how it dances;
its masquerades and its incursions.

And as I learn, a well within me deepens
and a suddenness of joy will sometimes come,
fresh from the dark water.

December 1998

Season of Grief

January cuts me
like an ice wind brings
the echo of your dying.

I begin my third spring
alone with the useless snowdrops
still pushing silently skywards.

February 2000

The Solitary Retreat

Three kinds of ink,
two small paint boxes,
a dozen books,
three kinds of incense,
a choice of teas,
chocolate and halva,
knitting,
a radio and tape player,
two maps,
a selection of dharma talks,
a whole transcribed tape-lecture series,
a bird book,
a tin whistle
and a torch.

And here I sit,
solitary,
entertained by the lichen on the tree,
fascinated by the sudden brightening of the sun.

September 1998

At the Margins

When I have fled
beyond all
that is reasonable

I find myself
at home
on the margins.

In that cold
is space.
In yawning terror

air enough
to breathe.
There too

small treasures
dropped
by slowing time.

That jagged stone,
a patch of moss,
these blades
of sharp,
green grass.

February 1999

Always

I always (always,
always, always)
wanted to get close

to life. As a child
I passed long afternoons
wondering intently how

to become and antirrhinum.
How to breathe the secret
of vanilla rain falling

on window panes for a whole
day. How to lie still enough
to nuzzle up close to the

earthy moment that it might
take me for a friend
and carry me high

through the stillness and silence
over the long pass deep
into the mountain of unknowing.

April 1999

The Rite of Fascination Comes First

Teller of dreams, did you see the sun arc that day?
The way its rays peered, incredulous, through the glass?

Did you hear that the rain gathered itself in a tightness of delight
before pouring tears of light upon the landscape?

Did you feel the shadows of your words steal away silently, and wait
in dark corners, so I could collect them and carry them home?

Did you smell the air that saved a space for us
and made out meaning from the music of our thoughts?

And did you touch the ground as I did, and feel it there,
deep and necessary – holding calmly the moment when we met?

June 1999

Transaction

Coming to buy eggs, you wear
the lacy hand-knit cardigan,
your camel-hair coat, good
shoes, a hat and orange lipstick.

Eighty-something and accustomed
to service, you stand waiting,
trusting the small unspoken
ritual that I will see.

I leave the till and come to help.
Choosing among the tray of eggs
as carefully as I would have chosen
for my own grandmother.

You expect no less of me.
Always, I ask how you are.
you reply evasively, politely
avoiding raw reality.

Praising your fortune,
you tell me about a brother
who drove a hundred miles
to see you, sick at Christmas.

Today, fresh back from visiting,
you say that you'll be leaving
and how you will miss people – me
and the lady at the bank who smiles.

June 1999

BRISTOL

Bridge from my past
Reaching into the present
It puzzles me, the way it pulls me back.
So long ago I cried in Clifton,
Tried to leave by many desperate means.
Over the gorge, the bridge hangs in silent suspension.
Loving its dangerous call, I return.

July 1999

From a Dhanakosa Window

Thursday, 7.30 am

I wanted to say
to the wind, stop
your relentless
shaking of the arms
of the young copper beech
can't you see how it holds
onto its leaves for dear life
wet and ragged
in the morning rain
don't you feel
its leaves will be there
so little time
they need better than this
or is it that they are
laughing and it is I
who cannot see?

June 2000

Web

A small brown spider
slung the quivering ropes
of her white web
from the seashell mobile I made,
to the driftwood bowl on the table
and out to a brown paper bag
of fabric, bought for trousers.

I worried at the investment of such labour
between three points of such uncertainty.
But it was begun. And I could only watch
the inward spiral. She climbed
from thread to thread, reached out
tiny crooked legs, twitched her body
to the side, fastened the threads.

Later, she hung still at the centre,
patient or exhausted, I supposed.
I prayed for flies, for something
as reward before the wind
or careless hands collapsed
this weightless, half seen
mesh of death and beauty

which holds my breath,
            catches the light,
                    and out of which
                            the spider never falls.

July 2000

At last the light

While the pages of your Gary Larson calendar make their way to the
rubbish
(except the good ones, which you save like hoarded laughter)
the days go on being days
and I keep shaking them to see what I can get out.

Tangled in the safety-net of a full mind, I forget I don't need the answer
to all the questions ever asked; the sky is always present
in puddles and the sea is there, in the glass, at the side of my bed.

I must plant a beginning deep in every moment. And bury it again,
and again and again in the darkness. Then I'll be free to feel
the way a poem feels when at last the light falls upon its page.

August 2000

i put paperclips on the loose ideas that clutter the porch

i remember how i used to think
that everyone kept the same ornaments
on the same shelves for twenty years

there is a kind of chaos that is longing for me

i catch it from the corner of my eye
then look away for the regularly placed
reassurance of street lamps

trees shout loudly to me that they can dance

and i'm obliged to let them,
until i can muster enough imagination
to make them stop

angels and archangels soar dangerously near my ears

all kinds of secrets bubble up from drains
in a surprising syntax of sudden messages
i find myself lost

the wind makes loud invisible shapes from the torn air

and what I feel is the cold
hand of inevitability trying to push me
down the path i'd always chosen

December 2000

Puzzle

There is a long afternoon ahead.
You are laying out the pieces of a puzzle –
edges on this side, middles on that.

After a while, you begin to suspect
it's not just one, but maybe three
different puzzles bought from Oxfam,

jumbled in a bag. Probably not all there.
And it seems like some bits
are never going to fit.

"Perhaps it would be best," you think,
"to throw away these ones.
They don't really go with the others.

It will make more room on the table.
I'll be able to see what's what."
And so you begin throwing them away.

They get mixed up with old apple cores,
used tissues, and the screwed up abandoned drafts
of poems in the copper waste paper bin under the table.

The puzzle goes fine all afternoon, then,
standing back, you gradually begin to see
the gaps. And the lack of pieces to fill them.

As you kneel down and begin to delve about
in the bin, you can't help marvelling
that one small puzzle could really fit in so much sky.

July 2001

The One-Armed Bandit

It reminded me of Aunty Con especially.
Her concentration. Handbag on arm,
wearing a white courtelle cardigan,
she fed coins into the full-moon slot,
pulled the handle, let it spring back.

We always hoped for a jackpot row
of oranges, blue plums or bar signs,
but mostly got the one, right hand, cherry
that gave you just 4p to keep you going
after every six or eight goes.

Now, thirty years on I found one, skulking
in the back corner of a Lyme Regis arcade
behind Star Wards machines, pin-ball tables
and the teetering 10p temptation of the "Penny Falls"
machine with its sign that said "Don't bang".

I meant to spend just loose coppers from my purse,
then changed down silver at a kiosk stacked with coins.
I was buying a feeling – being eight again. Washed
and dressed after tea for a holiday evening out, down
Creek Road, Hayling Island, sunburnt from the beach.

All through my body was a child's solemnity
as I pulled down the arm. And my mother's voice –
I couldn't quite hear it over the din –
was she telling me to pull it down slowly,
or was it to let it go, quick?

May 2001

On the train to Basingstoke

Opposite me, across the gangway, on the red-upholstered seats
sits a youngish man in a blue shirt. His feet are planted
squarely apart at the end of his navy blue trousers.
His blue tie has lilac and pale blue squares on it.
He wears small, metal-framed glasses.

On his knees he has a very slim lap-top computer and he talks
into a mobile telephone; about door details,
brush details – whether they can be glued to wooden doors because
they've always been routed-in before.
He is concerned about the white wall.

I wonder what he does on Sundays. There are creases
across the middle of his well-polished, black, leather shoes
like he crouches down a lot.
The inside pocket of his navy-blue jacket is frayed, showing
some white fabric. His brown hands now hold a pen firmly.

He is making decisive marks on the stapled sheets
resting on his diary. I notice that the pen is a propelling pencil.
He is called Matt. The train has stopped by a line of oak trees
with the sun shining down on them. Another train whistles past.
A child laughs. Somewhere behind me a cellophane wrapper rustles.

Matt shuffles his papers. We are on the move again.
He is called Matt Saunders. The sun is hot.
The train slows to a station. A small row
of old fashioned shops. West Byfleet. Cantilevered
training desks – the client wants to fit cable trays underneath.

He's phone to ask the price. They're 800 wide.
By the track, the leaves are dying from the edges inwards.
One has brown edges, then a part that's yellow,
before a perfectly green but shrinking centre.
We are miles down the track, stopped again, and again
there are oak trees.

September 2001

(Not Quite) Twenty Blessings

May the loch run deep into your heart.
May the wings of swifts carry your thoughts.
May the fresh smell of grass greet your homecoming.
May the music of the wind soothe your sleeping.
May the smell of pines hang behind your footsteps.
May refractions of light spread across your smile.
May the many unnamed trees teach you their essence.
May time slow to a curtsey as you pass.
May the day be long enough for all your dreaming.
May the night be wide enough to let you fly.
May the singing fish of winter haunt your sadness.
May the bright and speckled thrush delight your sky.
May the mountain pass kneel down to help you climb it.
May the forests part like water as you walk.
May clouds of rain and sunshine keep you nourished, and
May the day go slowly till we part.

June 1999